Brigitte's Blue Heart

BRIGITTE'S BLUE HEART

JEREMY REED

CRESCENT MOON

ENGLAND

CRESCENT MOON PUBLISHING
18 Chaddesley Road
KIDDERMINSTER
Worcestershire
DY 10 3AD U.K.

First published 1998
© Jeremy Reed 1998

Designed by Radiance Graphics, London
Printed in Great Britain
Set in Montype Bembo

British Library Cataloguing in Publication data

Reed, Jeremy
    Brigitte's blue heart. – (British Poets Series)
    I. Title
    821.9 14

    ISBN 1-86171-008-9

Reed, Jeremy
    Brigitte's blue heart. – Signed ed. – (British Poets Series)
    I. Title
    821.9 14

    ISBN 1-86171-009-7 (signed edition)

Contents

BARDOT

The blue jeaned pouty gamine. A pine cone
drops on the beach, *circa* 1960.
Her black bikini bottom warms like skin.

Age is the future walking on white stilts
into and out the sea. Sometimes an eye
will burn somebody in the crowd:

a look's a mark like the white patch
excluded from her tan. Blond hair flying

behind an open sportscar, dark glasses,
the moment hurts like a bee sting.
It smells of black petunias.

Now age is upfront. The myth loses wing,
the camera lens closes its eye
and dream. She thinks back to that afternoon
or one similar, blue on blue,
it's now or yesterday in inner time,
her body coppering, the coastal road

eaten so fast the car climbs to the sky.

CHARLES AZNAVOUR

Sometimes a voice cuts right into one's life,
it's like a spinal dye, a sensory
association with the little thing
dominant in a mood, green eyes
remembered in a café by the beach
or just some moment when an ambient blue
touched everything; I only feel this bad
when I'm collected by the past
as though a name was cut into my heart,
so too red lips, a telephone number
I'll remember even in death,

and that reflective lyric elegy,
the smoky pin in 'Yesterday When I Was Young',
each time autumn recurs, or I pick up
a token from our past, from everyone's
backlist of broken memories
poured like fine sand out of a shoe
kept in red tissue wrappers in a box.

And did he write that song, a whisky glass
placed on the piano-top, autumn outside
like a silk dress left in the park?
I listen to his voice, recall French films,
Bardot bobbing her blond hair, and his words
pour like a rich wine in the early dark.

STORMY WEATHER

Take me so bluely, greyly, stormily,
and always blackily, inconclusively,
into that bluesy, jazzy song,
it's Lena Horn, or Bille Holiday,
perhaps even Sinatra's rounding out
of love's moody, sad inequalities
I'm playing on this rainy day,

reflecting on old unrequited love
left like a red glove on the beach
for the highest wave to retrieve
and scoop into the frothy swash.
Don't easy couples marry on the beach? –

a black car standing by for a white dress
a black dress standing by for a white car.
Billie could find no equal in a man.

Pre-thunder clarity, and sassy pink
luminous under density
building as massive cumulus.
Something will break; a sonic riff

bring back the sharpest memories,
the ones that bite like lemon juice.

I play it over, 'Stormy Weather',
the way she gets the rhyme on 'together',
before the vampish hurt breaks through
gritty with memories, and the fast rain
orchestrates every shade of moody blue.

ARUM LILIES

Outmoded in their funeral part
rococco decoratioin for the dead
in ivy-blackened cemeteries, they're now
significant in Robert Mapplethorpe's
up-fronted flower shots, or as stemmed backdrop
accoutrements to fashion shoots,
a lily flopping like a sail
gone dead for lack of breezy push

in the cloudless, blue afternoon.
A lily open like a concert hall
dominated by a tall orange microphone.

My 6 are 5 with one given away.
They bring a meditative calm
to the flat's nervy ambience.
They're like siestas in a dusty town.
White psychic stuff inside the head.

No need to choreograph their way,
their poise is exact, lazy roll
towards a point in gravity.
I go with their roomed life-expectancy,
attend their heavy gowns, a week or two,
and stars blaze outside in the windy night.

KNOCKING ON HEAVEN'S DOOR

After the damage, its castrati sing,
of restoration and the nutrient orchestra
reviving health. I kept apart
a whole autumn, while scarlet leaves
basked on wet surfaces like carp
up from the sedimental depth.
Dreams touched me with the greater clarity;

shine on and on and brightly shine.
Once when I crossed a field, I saw a man,
an oval mirror for a head,
a black jacket, and the name Lautréamont
written on the polished surface.

And this blue door, its paint flaking,
I knock on it down an alley,
and hear on the other side, is it clouds

flying across a sonic roar
deep as the wild baritone-grating autumn sea?

NIGHT PEOPLE

Out of your mouth I retrieved a red thread
vibrant with discourse from the underworld,
your tongue injecting sensory data

into my own. Once they discovered gold
beyond the mountain range, travelled at night
to keep the secret. Now I work
the night as day as naturally
as how you disengage a shoe
to place a foot on my shoulder
another form of nocturnal vocabulary.

Proust worked all night. The traffic dead outside.
I like to hear itinerant taxis
policing the dark, and your red thread
pulsing with sexual narrative

leads me where, black-eyed, glowering, you sit up
heady with expectation on the bed.

EVEN COWGIRLS GET THE BLUES

A saxophone is wailing underground,
a jazzy coda to the equinox
which lay exhausted like a red dragon,
belly open, spilling rich leaves,
blotchy and black and shining in the grass,
her washed out Levis hanging upside down
like a blue melon on stretch legs,
she fits them like her skin was airbrushed blue.

She waits to hear him call, and say 'Sarah,
the future's there behind your eyes,
be blindfold for a minute in the car,
that's letting go as though the seconds ticked
towards a vertical cliff edge,'

and then he hangs up, she takes in her jeans,
the red backpocket patch shaped like a star.

ANGEL

The night's a dark blue door open into the night,
an empty room in which the silence blows
like wind out of a film. And your white dress

has been exchanged for black; the stars
are one blaze burning up in the mirror.
If death's an end-point to biography,
it seem less that an hour before dawn,
your stockings breathing at the knee
in shivers, configurations
writing a nocturnal vocabulary

with each transference of movement to silk.
What did we hear as a nocturnal pitch,
a wolf, a chimera come above ground,
or a jazz singer's spliffed phrasing,
words escaped like a smoky pearl?

We wait for dawn: a red bridge in the sky,
the dead on it waving their flags
out of the clouds. We'll come together then,
and celebrate the morning star

and how a poem escapes on your fevered cry.

INTIMATE CONFESSIONS

You sit in silence. Suspended delay
like thunder building behind the cloud-line,
static quirky with energies.

You cross your legs and it's like cutting silk.
Once I picked up bright sunlight in a barn
and carried it like a gold bar
out of the dark back to the light.

I tell you small inconsequential things
like how Billie Holiday dyed her pubic hair
nasturtium-red. Nasturtiums splash
the garden with Kimono prints,
shocking, peppery, red cartwheels.

When you confide, I hear the dark
unconscious open like a lake
returning a sunk boat to the surface.
You sit in it and row deliberately
across the calm, and word by word
set out for the opposite shore, and I

collect the ripples fanning out and free.

MOVE RIGHT IN

A ferroconcrete bunker, grey carpets,
monitors recessed into walls,
Madonna's HQ, or the standard kit
for sometime future survival, the sea
pushes in a white table, later chairs
across a mile of razzled beach. A town
slipped with the coast, a tectonic relapse
in the fortified colony.
Somewhere a videophone blips alive
on a glass-topped desk, and a red orchid
retrieves the call. Platinum discs are badged

the length of an underground corridor.
Today's tomorrow. The pink fridge is stacked
with champagne, nutrient drinks, food capsules.
Concealed vaults bank Erotica out-takes,
software archives, survival manuals
should too much violet leak through, or the sea
solidify with toxic waste. Outside,
a pilot in a gold rhinestoned jacket
attends the heliport. We make out way
through brainfade towns, and meet up with the
                                                    shore,
and find a bungalow washed in,
white, pristine like a yacht, a clapboard monument

to other times, the ones we left,
in coming here, and decided to stay.

BLUE LOU

I know that title somewhere, it's a song
circa 1930, the jazzation
afforded a voice bluesy as a horn.
Today, the title's onomatopoeia
brings to my mind the modern skies we've known
no counting the decades since Ashbery
jump-started a new poetry.
Blues as a jeans shade, and an abstract tone
seen like the future through a smoked window.

Day in day out I try to read
a meaning on the other side of light.
Your letter came the sooner for my need,
opening it had your voice jump in the room.

Sometimes my solitude's like depth
I'll never measure with my hand.
A place down there. The waters break
if the diver jumps flat.

I wait for you to telephone
a year away, a future call
from time I've never reached. You'll tell me how
the changes have occurred, and what I'll find
when I arrive, your house is painted white,
it's blue today with creeper on one wall.

VIOLENT NARCISSUS

It's always Tuesday when the orange car
negotiates a leafy parking spot.
They go inside and open up the house,
she wearing a black wedding dress
and he carrying white roses.
'Sometimes it rains inside a dream,'
he says, 'The big spot like a music score,
staves, crochets, beading like black feet
suspended from a washing-line,'

or so I like to imagine
because they seem peculiar,
her black wedding dress and his orange car.
What they do inside is a short story,
the one I'll come to write in time, they keep

all curtains drawn, but in the back garden
he tinkers with his model cars,
miniature, glossy veterans, it's his fix,
blue, green and red fetishes. She comes out
minus her wedding dress and points
to something going over in a cloud,

a pink cloud shaped like Africa
cat-napping on its side. And when they're gone,

I imagine their night, he driving fast
towards a restaurant in the forest,
the white roses held on his lap
and both discoursing on their varied past.

HYACINTHS

The whorled ribcase
a smoky scent that bites at memory
so tangy that it turns the head
of an old love affair, small mouth

redly printed across my neck,
blond hair blown out of a French film.
Two blue, a pink, a pristine white,
topheavy coiffures in a bowl

they're like long sentences in Proust
strung into noodled cones
expansive as pasta.
Their thick stems live like green fish in water.

Mostly I come on them in bursts,
a flash travelling through the room
that sometimes centres attention
until they are the focal point,

a heady, vibrant punctum.
What if they spoke with a vocabulary
I understood, parallelled words,
would I survive that frequency?

Sometimes from a perverse instinct
I imagine a pink one zipped
into a slinky skirt, a blue
dramatic in a tuxedo.

They force a way into my life
hooking at sensory stimuli
four mythopoeic stylised beehives
cool as a girlie Motown group from the sixties.

THE SHOP AT THE END OF THE WORLD

Rumoured to have green shutters and white walls,
much like a harbour cafe, no one in
or ever answerable to the ships
which stop off in the bay, petrol-tankers,
cargo-lines, all the big vessels
that roll by like floating hotels, sound off
and headed somewhere else, go by
as punctuation marks on the blank trip,
a dead-end place, a mirage suspended
beneath the mountain, or a trapped image
isolated on a blue TV screen,
it's a probable fixture, mussel shell
cracked on the red upholstery
inside the one abandoned car
parked out of gunshot of the waves

collapsing in slow dazzle on the beach.
They say the occupier's various,
a space cadet, a sailor who turned gold,
or someone working at a software kill
for six years as a single night.
A depot, outpost, utility store
for rum and cigarettes, or a recess
for programming security data,
we'll never know its purpose, but keep watch

for it to meet our view one random day
of interminable latitude,
when what was to be a brief coastal hop
deepened to a voyage with islands slipping by
and big calms nosing in, and suddenly
it's whitely visible, the mountain too
with its flag of volcanic smoke
writing a question on the empty sky.

THE DISPOSSESSED

I carry autumns buried in my heart,
red leaves turned over black, a rainy tang
of seasonal dissolution, and the stag
has dropped gold antlers in the lake,
the dead increased their number on the microfiche,
a continuous incremental elegy
goes with their passage through the underworld
to a big empty room, where a low blues
smokes from the singer's throat, as though a voice
crossed from the deep South to her abdomen
in the space of a breath. Or does she breathe
or sing direct from consciousness?
The dead sleepwalking through transparently,
following one clue then the next
like bees directed to a honey jar
left uncapped in the kitchen. Every year
the sense of outlawed dispossession grows,
we're moving away from the source to where?
An empty cafe in the wood,
a jittery departure lounge after midnight,
the flight again delayed for autumn fog.
I study faces for their sense of loss,
the nervous highways routed through the dark
in search of a consolatory hotel,
Heartbreak Hotel lit bluely in the night,

and we're all headed to a foreign space,
a dispossession of identity,
no subway ticket, just the silent strain
of waiting for a friend, a sort of guide
to telescope a way towards the light.

MONKSHOOD

Suitably darker tones than indigo,
a thunder sky reflected in a lake
roofed over by dense trees. Our high ladder
lost legs after you went too far
and dropped the glass word we had kept
hidden for future retrieval.
A curtain's drawn across the horizon
each time I contemplate a life
without you as its centre. When I hear
the singer a-cappella, and the note
is bruised, but hits the purple spot,
I think of monkshood or bitter coffee
stripping defences by its scent.
I let go, and a road leads dustily
towards a house stepped back from a quarry
from which occasionally someone appears
carrying a thought in their hands
that's busy like an animal.
Dark tone again. The black petunia
a tortoise bites in a garden, and now
a clearer indicator, words that beat
persistently at paper walls, and break
sense barriers. I close my eyes, count three,
the flowers take a breather in the hall.

ALLEYCAT BLUES

She fires herself up on mean housebreaking,
catsuited Zoe slamming a blue van
through alleys in the deep night, hair tied back,
her features tight with recrimination,
her face made up for each precise

articulated raid. She never lost,
dipping in and out of waterfront flats,
her tyre-marks left as an insignia
rubbered across a landing bay,

she made the harbours her nocturnal site.
Daytime she slept behind drawn blinds,
hennaed her hair geranium-red,
called up a girlfriend, configurated
ways to walk clean through a brick wall

like white psychic phenomena.
She lived in rhythm with the underworld,
but for an hour each day choreographed
her dance-steps in the brilliant light,
perfect somatic symmetry,

blinds open, in red ballet shoes,
then returned to her discourse with the night,

felt her excitement start to build

around a number on its sea-view height.

BILLIE HOLIDAY AND RAINY SUNDAYS

for John Robinson

The long extended leisure of a blue Sunday,
a rainy one with all living deferred
like an escape back to a childhood loft
for discourse without adults, secrecy
in taking out forbidden magazines
and the elliptic orange juggling balls,
Sunday a distillation of high light,
a panoramic eye-piece to flat clouds.
I swear a red canoe flew through the sky.

And now it means a chill out from the drive
forcing adrenalin all week,
time to rediscover intimate needs,
and savour Billie Holiday's
drug-loaded, half cut phrasing, bluesy pain
sung as a loser's confession,
she never wins, but celebrates her loss
as loyalty, the walk out cause to sing
and reason to be Lady Day.
Where does the person hurt inside the song
go in the late hours, do they board a train,
a red train headed way down South?
And do they start again in some hotel
called Sleepy Time Down South? Billie's bruised
                              notes

make long distance connections in the heart,
this rainy Sunday when I'm staying home,
listening to "I Cover the Waterfront",
and learning to live my solitary part.

DARK GREEN BERET

Worn at a slant, not paramilitary,
but chic by association,
the young Bardot, or camply questioning
by angles how a stylish archetype
brings Paris straight to mind, a made-up eye
which could have jumped out of a blue Miro
arresting by a profile. Later fog.

The fineness in your face today
establishes links with my past,
my island harbours, Leonard Cohen's songs
in all their agonized transparency
having me think a blue raincoat
could only be a Burberry.
I used to watch the sculptures in the mist
individuate like shirts on hangers,
an orange sun came polishing
all that blowy phenomena.

Now, I'm more grown into my life,
the years collect like medals on my coat,
although I've lost the means to read
their many tarnished inscriptions.
Your wearing a simple dark green beret
leaves me needing a pianist to lay down

the sadness that I feel, and yesterday
was that an hour ago, with ships calling
out in the bay, and I just beginning
to learn what brings me down, what brings me
                          down.

SIMPLE LITTLE THINGS

Poetry in your nerves like sugar rot,
social dysfunction. And the wind flops dead,
there' no one in it, like television,
an uninhabited technocracy.

Cheesecake or strawberry gateau in the dark
to enhance flavour. You're alone
sitting inside a rotund vowel

like a red rocking chair.
A haiku is the shortest route

of travelling, some simple little thing
got in the hand like a violet tattoo.

EUROPEAN WRITERS

German Romantic Poetry: Goethe, Novalis,
Heine, Hölderlin, Schlegel, Schiller
by Carol Appleby

Cavafy: Anatomy of a Soul
by Matt Crispin

Rilke: Space, Essence and Angels in the Poetry of Rainer Maria Rilke
by B.D. Barnacle

Rimbaud: Arthur Rimbaud and the Magic of Poetry
by Jeremy Robinson

Petrarch, Dante and the Troubadours: The Religion of Love and Poetry
by Cassidy Hughes

Dante Studies: Dante in Love: The Vita Nuova
by Joanna Finn-Kelcey

Dante: Selections From the Vita Nuova
translated by Thomas Okey

Arthur Rimbaud: Selected Poems
edited and translated by Andrew Jary

Arthur Rimbaud: A Season in Hell
edited and translated by Andrew Jary

Gide: Fiction and Fervour
by Jeremy Robinson

Samuel Beckett Goes Into the Silence
by Jeremy Robinson

In the Dim Void; Samuel Beckett's Late Trilogy
by Gregory Johns

Friedrich Hölderlin: Selected Poems
translated by Michael Hamburger

Sappho: *Poems*
translated by J.M. Edmonds

Hélène Cixous: I Love You: The Jouissance of Writing
by Kelly Ives

Luce Irigaray: Lips, Kissing & the Politics of Sexual Difference
by Kelly Ives

Julia Kristeva: Art, Love, Melancholy, Philosophy, Psychoanalysis
by Kelly Ives

Forthcoming:
individual studies of: Arthur Rimbaud; Rainer Maria Rilke;
André Gide; Novalis; Friedrich Hölderlin